DOGS SET VIII

BOSTON TERRIERS

Jill C. Wheeler
ABDO Publishing Company

visit us at
www.abdopublishing.com

Published by ABDO Publishing Company, 8000 West 78th Street, Edina, Minnesota 55439. Copyright © 2010 by Abdo Consulting Group, Inc. International copyrights reserved in all countries. No part of this book may be reproduced in any form without written permission from the publisher. The Checkerboard Library™ is a trademark and logo of ABDO Publishing Company.

Printed in the United States of America, North Mankato, Minnesota.
092009
012010

♻ PRINTED ON RECYCLED PAPER

Cover Photo: Alamy
Interior Photos: Alamy p. 19; Getty Images pp. 5, 9, 13, 17, 21; iStockphoto p. 7;
     Photolibrary pp. 11, 15

Series Coordinator: Tamara L. Britton
Editors: Heidi M.D. Elston, BreAnn Rumsch
Art Direction: Neil Klinepier

Library of Congress Cataloging-in-Publication Data

Wheeler, Jill C., 1964-
  Boston terriers / Jill C. Wheeler.
    p. cm. -- (Dogs)
  Includes index.
  ISBN 978-1-60453-782-6
  1. Boston terrier. I. Title.
  SF429.B7W44 2010
  636.72--dc22
                              2009036369

CONTENTS

The Dog Family 4

Boston Terriers 6

What They're Like 8

Coat and Color 10

Size 12

Care 14

Feeding 16

Things They Need 18

Puppies 20

Glossary 22

Web Sites 23

Index 24

THE DOG FAMILY

It is hard to imagine life without dogs. Humans and dogs have lived together for thousands of years. Researchers believe the first dogs were wolf pups humans used as hunting companions.

Over time, humans **bred** these animals to maintain or improve certain qualities. Today, we have more than 400 different dog breeds. All dogs are members of the family **Canidae**. They share many features, including keen senses of smell and hearing.

In early times, humans bred dogs to fight. This practice continues to this day. However, most people now find dogfighting cruel.

One of today's most friendly dog breeds can trace its roots back to fierce fighting ancestors. That breed is the Boston terrier.

The Boston terrier (left) is one of the few dog breeds native to the United States.

BOSTON TERRIERS

The Boston terrier **breed** began around 1870 in Boston, Massachusetts. At that time, Boston resident Robert Hooper bought an imported dog named Judge. Judge was part English bulldog and part English terrier. Soon, Boston residents began breeding similar bulldog and terrier crosses.

Fans of this new cross called their dogs bull terriers or round heads. In 1889, they organized the American Bull Terrier Club. However, bull terrier and bulldog fans opposed the new name. They did not want their breeds to share a name with such a different dog.

The club changed its name to the Boston Terrier Club of America in 1891. At that time, the members established the name *Boston terrier* for their dogs.

In 1893, the **American Kennel Club (AKC)** recognized the Boston terrier as a **breed**. This was the first time the AKC recognized a breed developed entirely in the United States.

The Boston terrier is the state dog of Massachusetts.

What They're Like

The Boston terrier is nicknamed the American Gentleman for its wonderful temperament. The **breed** is gentle and well mannered.

Boston terriers are enthusiastic, playful, and come in a small package. They make excellent companions and great family pets. Boston terriers do well with everyone, including small children. Their limited exercise needs make them suitable for houses or apartments.

These small dogs are intelligent and easy to train. So, Boston terriers can take on special jobs. Their loving nature makes them excellent therapy dogs. They comfort people in hospitals, nursing homes, and assisted-living homes.

Boston terriers are small and friendly. They usually rank in the top 20 favorite breeds in the United States!

COAT AND COLOR

It is easy to recognize a Boston terrier because of its coat. The front of this dog's chest is white. This makes it look as though the dog is wearing a little **tuxedo**.

Boston terriers have white markings on a black, brindle, or seal coat. Brindle is a mixture of colors. Seal looks like black, but it has reddish tones in sunlight.

The white markings include a band on the **muzzle**. There should also be a **blaze** between the eyes.

Boston terriers have a single coat of smooth, short hair. This makes them easy to groom. But, they need help staying warm in cold temperatures.

The Boston terrier's tuxedo markings set this breed apart from others!

Booties will protect their feet from snow and cold. Sweaters or coats will also help them stay comfortable.

11

SIZE

Boston terriers are compact, sturdy dogs. They do well in small apartments or large houses. Full-grown Boston terriers usually stand 15 to 17 inches (38 to 43 cm) tall.

The **AKC** recognizes three weight classes for Boston terriers. The smallest dogs weigh less than 15 pounds (7 kg). The second class is for dogs weighing 15 pounds to less than 20 pounds (9 kg). The largest class is for Boston terriers that weigh 20 pounds up to 25 pounds (11 kg).

When choosing a Boston terrier, size is a matter of personal preference.

CARE

Boston terriers are pleasantly easy to care for. Their short coats require just a weekly brushing and an occasional bath. Owners should keep their Boston terrier's nails very trim. And, they need to regularly clean their dog's ears and teeth.

Owners will also need to find a veterinarian they trust. The veterinarian will keep the dog current on **vaccines**. And, he or she will check for health problems. The veterinarian can also **spay** or **neuter** Boston terriers.

Like bulldogs, the Boston terrier has a short **muzzle**. This can lead to breathing problems. Grunting and snoring are common with this **breed**.

These breathing problems mean Boston terriers have a hard time cooling themselves down. So, owners need to keep this dog from getting too hot.

Grooming is a great way for owners to spend quality time with their beloved dogs!

FEEDING

Diets are just as important to dogs as they are to people. Dogs need a high-quality food to give them energy every day.

Dog food can be dry, semimoist, or canned. Some owners prefer to make their own dog food from fresh ingredients. However, this is not advised without first talking to a veterinarian.

Since the Boston terrier has a short **muzzle**, it often takes in air while eating. So, owners should be prepared to live with a gassy dog.

In addition to food, Boston terriers need plenty of fresh water. This is especially important on warm days since these dogs overheat easily.

Owners should feed their Boston terriers at the same time every day.

THINGS THEY NEED

Boston terriers are active dogs that love to play with their owners. Daily walks and games of fetch are favorite forms of exercise. For more fun, Boston terriers can join organized sports with their owners.

It is best to avoid exposing Boston terriers to extreme temperatures. These dogs should not be outside when it is really hot or cold. Luckily, owners can exercise small Boston terriers indoors.

Before their new dog arrives, owners will need the right supplies. These include food and water bowls and a crate. Boston terriers also love a soft bed to sleep on. A collar, a license, and identification tags are also important. And, owners should purchase a brush, a comb, nail clippers, and toys.

Boston terriers need lots of love and play!

PUPPIES

Boston terrier puppies are delightful bundles of affectionate energy! But they require special attention. Owners will need to puppy proof their home before their new pet arrives. That means removing things a puppy might choke on or poisons it might swallow.

Boston terriers are smart dogs that learn quickly. When your Boston terrier is two to five months old, take it to puppy kindergarten. There, the puppy will learn important obedience skills.

Additional training will build your dog's skills. It can also help avoid problem behaviors. These include digging, excessive barking, and chewing.

It is best to buy a Boston terrier from a reputable **breeder**. With proper care, these lovable dogs will live for 10 to 13 years.

Most female dogs carry their puppies for about 63 days. The puppies are born blind and deaf. About 10 to 14 days after birth, their ear canals and eyes begin to open.

GLOSSARY

American Kennel Club (AKC) - an organization that studies and promotes interest in purebred dogs.

blaze - a usually white stripe down the center of an animal's face.

breed - a group of animals sharing the same ancestors and appearance. A breeder is a person who raises animals. Raising animals is often called breeding them.

Canidae (KAN-uh-dee) - the scientific Latin name for the dog family. Members of this family are called canids. They include domestic dogs, wolves, jackals, foxes, and coyotes.

muzzle - an animal's nose and jaws.

neuter (NOO-tuhr) - to remove a male animal's reproductive organs.

spay - to remove a female animal's reproductive organs.

tuxedo - a semiformal evening suit for men.

vaccine (vak-SEEN) - a shot given to animals or humans to prevent them from getting an illness or a disease.

WEB SITES

To learn more about Boston terriers, visit ABDO Publishing Company on the World Wide Web at **www.abdopublishing.com**. Web sites about Boston terriers are featured on our Book Links page. These links are routinely monitored and updated to provide the most current information available.

INDEX

A
American Bull
 Terrier Club 6,
 7
American Kennel
 Club 7, 12

B
bed 18
booties 11
Boston Terrier Club
 of America 7
breeder 20
brush 18

C
Canidae (family) 4
character 4, 8, 18,
 20
chest 10
coat 10, 14
collar 18
color 10
comb 18
crate 18

E
ears 14
exercise 8, 18
eyes 10

F
feet 11
fighting 4
food 16, 18

G
grooming 10, 14

H
health 14, 16
history 4, 6, 7
Hooper, Robert 6

L
license 18
life span 20

M
Massachusetts 6
muzzle 10, 14, 16

N
nail clippers 18
nails 14
neuter 14

P
puppies 20

S
size 8, 12
spay 14
sweaters 11

T
teeth 14
toys 18
training 8, 20

V
vaccines 14
veterinarian 14, 16

W
water 16, 18
work 8